THE LAST YELLOW ROSE

THE LAST YELLOW ROSE

LIN MARSHALL BRUMMELS

SANDHILLS PRESS / THE PLAINSWOMAN SERIES

NACOGDOCHES, TEXAS / ORD, NEBRASKA

Any correspondence should be addressed to:

The Editors
Sandhills Press
2274 FM 226
Nacogdoches, TX 75691

sandersmetx@gmail.com

Book design is by Mark Sanders and Kimberly Verhines.

ISBN 978-0-911015-49-2

Sandhills Press was founded by Mark Sanders at Ord, Nebraska, in 1979. Over the years, the Press has relocated to Missouri, Oklahoma, Idaho, and Texas; the Press, however, has remained rooted to its home state and continues to publish authors from Nebraska and the Plains. Since 1979, Sandhills Press and its subsidiary imprints, the Main-Traveled Roads Chapbook Series, the Plains Poetry Series, and Lewis-Clark Press, have published dozens of authors and books.

The Plainswoman Series is so-named after Kathleene West's book of poems, *Plainswoman: Her First Hundred Years,* which the Press published in 1985 as the first volume in the Plains Poetry Series. The Plainswoman Series honors the late Kathleene West for her contritubitons to Plains poetry and the legacy she created for marginalized women writers of the region forty years ago.

CONTENTS

II.

III.

For Liz

ACKNOWLEDGMENTS

This collection honors the family women who came before me and my talented daugher Elizabeth Della (Liz) born in 1984.

Della Mae Akers Marshall	B. 1881, M. 1904, D. 1953
Daisy Mae Branen West	B. 1889, M. 1914, D. 1959
Dorothy Mae West Marshall	B. 1920, M. 1945, D. 2002

Thank you to the following journals and magazines for publishing these poems or earlier versions of the poems. I would like to offer my gratitude to the artists and editors who read and offered suggestions regarding the poems in this collection. I would also like to say thank you, thank you, to those who wrote the generous blurbs for this book.

"Angels," "I Feel Sorry for the Other Mothers," "Wild Yellow Rose," *Fine Lines.*

"Closed Barn Doors," "Interchangeable," *The Power of the Feminine I, Anthology* (Thrush Press, 2023).

"Iris Garden," *Nebraska Life*, 2018.

"Leaning into Tomorrow," *Real Women Write, Beyond Covid: Leaning Into Tomorrow* (Story Circle Network, 2021).

"Letter to My 16-Year-Old Self," *Celebrate* (University of Nebraska-Omaha, Omaha, NE, 2014).

"Nerves," "Twins," *Cottonwood Strong* (Finishing Line Press, Georgetown, Kentucky, 2019).

"Progeny," "Yellowing Curtains," *Real Women Write, Seeing Through*

Their Eyes (Story Circle Network, 2022).

"Primary," "Chop Suey," *Real Women Write and Mentors: The Art of Nurturing* (Story Circle Network, 2022).

"She Won a Purple Ribbon," "Church Ladies," *A Quilted Landscape* (Scurfpea Publishing, Sioux Falls, South Dakota, 2021).

"Sour Cream Raisin," "Cherry Pie for Breakfast," *Kitchen Table Stories: Sharing Our Lives in Food* (Story Circle Network, 2022).

"Sweet Warmth," *Heron Clan XI* (Katherine James Books, 2024).

"Unwanted Beauty," "It's Not the End," "Home Early or Not at All," *A Safe and Brave Space* (Garden of Neuro Sisters and Friends, 2022).

INTRODUCTION

"Life is made of ever so many partings welded together."
Great Expectations
–Charles Dickens

Some of the poems in this collection reference genetic or health conditions. The brief definitions below are not intended to be comprehensive. Visit these and related websites for more information.

Genetics is the scientific study of genes and heredity; the study of how certain qualities or traits are passed from parents to offspring as a result of changes in DNA sequence. Source: National Institute of Health (NIH): https://www.nigms.nih.gov/education/fact-sheets/Pages/genetics.aspx.

A pedigree in genetics, is a chart that diagrams the inheritance of a trait or health condition through generations of a family. The pedigree shows the relationships among family members and, when the information is available, indicates which individuals have a trait(s) of interest. Source: National Institute of Health (NIH): https://www/genome.gov/genetics-glossary/Pedigree.

Phenylketonuria (fen-ul-key-toe-NU-ree-uh),(PKU) is a rare inherited disorder that causes an amino acid called phenylalanine to build up in the body. People with PKU need to follow a diet that limits phenylalanine, which is found mostly in foods that contain protein. Although there is no cure for PKU, recognizing it and starting treatment right away can help prevent limitations of thinking, understanding, and communicating (intellectual disability) and major health problems. Source: Mayo Clinic: https://www.mayoclinic.org/diseases-conditions/phenylketonuria/symptoms-causes/syc-20376302.

Epigenomics is a field in which researchers chart the locations and understand the functions of all the chemical tags that mark the genome. Source: National Institute of Health (NIH): https://www.genome.gov/about-genomics/fact-sheets/Epigenomics-Fact-Sheet.

Roseola is a generally mild infection that usually affects children by age 2. Roseola is so common that most children have been infected with roseola by the time they enter kindergarten. A child could have a convulsion (febrile seizure) if his or her fever becomes high or spikes quickly. Source: Mayo Clinic: https://www.mayoclinic.org/diseases-conditons/roseola/symptoms-causes/syc-20377283.

Celiac disease, sometimes called celiac sprue or gluten-sensitive enteropathy, is an immune reaction to eating gluten, a protein found in wheat, barley, and rye. Source: https://www.mayoclinic.org/diseases-conditions/celiac-disease/symptoms-causes/syc-20352220.

Double Helix, as related to genomics, is a term used to describe the physical structure of DNA. A DNA molecule is made up of two linked strands that wind around each other to resemble a twisted ladder in a helix-like shape. Each strand has a backbone made of alternating sugar (deoxyribose) and phosphate groups. Attached to each sugar is one of four bases: adenine (A), cytosine (C), guanine (G) or thymine (T). The two strands are connected by chemical bonds between the bases: adenine bonds with thymine, and cytosine bonds with guanine. Source: National Institute of Health (NIH): https://www.genome.gov/genetics-glossary/Double-Helix.

Anneals, a scientific term, is used to describe the joining of two complementary strands of nucleic acid. To cause two complementary strands of nucleic acid (such as DNA or RNA) to join by hydrogen bonding. During repair of DNA double-strand breaks, cells must accurately anneal broken strands. Also: to induce the binding of a genetic primer to a complementary single-stranded nucleic acid by slowly cooling single strands obtained from the heating and separation of double-stranded DNA or RNA. Source: Merriam Webster Dictionary.

I.

Your Story

If you invest in beauty, it will remain with you all the days of your life.
—Frank Lloyd Wright

Be fearless and authentic, tell
your story, drop your anxiety
in a bucket, empty it into the wind,
let troubles fly away.

Light a lamp illuminating dark
corners where fears hide. They
wait for the right moment to return,
flee when you shine.

Stand strong against unfair
folks, rules, and legal dictates.
Don't be afraid of past mistakes,
forgive yourself.

Become the person you admire,
let your wild love light the way,
get organized, begin the day
with a smile, share your talents.

Slay dragons blocking your path,
your story is a journey tale,
walking the rough road to become.
This is my story too.

Leaning Into Tomorrow

My post-WWII parents
lost hope in the future;
no money to buy good land,
renting poor farm ground,
always owing the bank,
butchering mortgaged hogs
to feed the kids,
one son lost to mental illness
another son dies too young.

I look back at those yesterdays,
start to fall,
just in time catch hold
of a bit of moonlight
revealing the rocky path
to travel when moving
beyond what I believe to be
my broken family

They were no doubt like
many poor farm families
trying to scratch a living
in sandy soil
that should have been left
as native grass
in the great Sandhills.

Leaning into tomorrow
I regain balance,
stumble along
a path toward sunrise;
see wind towers

sprouting from fertile ground
that used to grow crops,
land my parents
would have loved.

Even on foggy days
when the way is murky,
like today,
I embrace the future,
know sun will shine
on my imperfect life.

4

Twins

For my cousin Nancy

Our twin mothers didn't look or act alike
but were each half of a whole
like a grapefruit split for breakfast,
my aunt kind and sweet, covered in sugar,
mom, acidic with pre-cut sections salted.

I was a bit salty like my mama, my cousin
sugary like hers. We were only girls among
seven brothers. I wanted to be pretty like her.
We were sisters in our hearts, hiked the hills
and valleys near her home and dreamed.

She moved after high school
and we lost track. Mom said my cousin
became a model, hoped the same for me.

My aunt kept house for a doctor,
raised his nine kids after her own
until Auntie's breast cancer diagnosis
forced early retirement. Mother's
better angel died when she lost her twin.
Twenty years later a tumor took Mom too.

I learned my cousin was a model-secretary;
Mom had only heard part of the story,
created her own conclusion as was her way.

My cousin, raised old school, quit work
when she married. We reconnected
after thirty years, became Facebook friends
and exchange Christmas cards,
today's version of walking the hills.

Reuse and Repurpose

My mom, second born of twin girls
in 1920, grew up in the thirties when people
never bought new, learned to reuse
and repurpose like many today without
jobs or homes, must do. After dad died
she lived on a Social Security check
leaving her eligible for food subsidies
she didn't want. Mom must have gone
to every garage sale in her town then,
bought everything she could get for a buck;
toys, knickknacks, kitchen utensils. She
brought them to me even though I said no.
I dream of my dead mother, delivering
a broken sewing machine to me, though
I tell her no. Twenty years gone, and even
in my dreams she never listens.

I insist I don't want it, still use the one
she and Dad gave me for a high school
graduation gift. There's no actual space
in my nook for another machine,
yet in the dream, sewing room is a big sunny
space where my old machine and a newer
Bernina machine are already set up
and ready to go. I'll discard her broken one
like I got rid of commodities powdered milk
by feeding it to feral cats, and threw
out her garage sale finds after each visit.
My brothers and I cleared her house
after she passed, and disposed of a life's
accumulation of empty whipped topping bowls,
old appliance boxes, and plastic bread bags,
saved just in case there's no money to buy new.
We ignore the lessons of living without
in a busted economy to our peril.

Rosie Years

My maternal grandmother was a teacher and wanted her children to have an education like she did. Her twin daughters started high school like their older sister before them when our country was in the throes of the Great Depression. The family was poor and lived too far from town to walk to school. Each of the twins lived with a different family during their high school years. My mother's job was as a live-in maid and babysitter in exchange for her room and board. She did all the family's laundry, cleaned their house, and helped prepare meals to pay her way. She was up at five every morning to finish chores before classes. Her twin sister's host family treated her like a daughter, didn't require her labor. The three girls worked hard, graduated from high school in an era when many had to quit school and work. Mom labored on her father's farm helping plant and harvest crops, until her younger brother was old enough to do farm work. They used a team of horses to plant and cultivate fields, then picked corn by hand in autumn. Mother did not speak happily of those times. Farming required hard labor. Days were long, and her hands bled from husking the dry ears of corn. Mom left farming behind during WWII to work in Nebraska's defense plants. She toiled in two different factories building bombs to support the war effort, lived with other young women in dormitories near those factories. This time of working outside the home and earning income was particularly important to her. She kept her pay stubs from that time in a safe deposit box her entire life. It was her sole paid work, but she never talked about bomb-making or the other women she met during her "Rosie the Riveter" years.

Closed Barn Doors

Harley was alternatively kind and hard
so, the story goes, spent lavishly
on himself but denied those

nearest. He always had a new car,
fine clothes, bought ice cream
and candy for the neighbor kids

wanting others to see his generosity,
but the family lived like paupers
in a tiny house without plumbing.

Vicky married first, then Dora.
Mom was the last sister to leave,
finally married her soldier after WW II.

She told stories about times Harley
took her and her sisters
to the barn to discipline them.

Pressed for details, she always
answered, *Daddy just tickled us girls.*

When Harley was elderly yet still able
to drive he visited often, always sitting
by the only door between kitchen and parlor.

When I walked by, he grabbed at me.
I learned to jerk away like it was a fire drill,
run past as fast as I could,

knowing he was too old to chase me
unlike Mom who believed his lies
and didn't know how to get away.

Sex Education

Mom confined her sex ed talk
to topics that affected her
like a hen protecting her nest.
My first blood arrived
year I turned twelve,
catching me unaware and not
knowing why I was bleeding.
Sorting laundry before Monday's
wash day she found bloody
underwear where I tossed them
too embarrassed to ask what to do.
*You're big enough to clean
your soiled panties now,* she squawked,
tossed them to me across the kitchen.
Mom begrudged money for pads,
wanted me to use rolled-up rags
that could be reused like she did.
A sister-in-law gave me a tampon
when I was a green kid of thirteen.
I didn't know to remove
cardboard covering, tried
inserting the whole thing, sitting
carefully until cardboard softened,
wishing for a pillow,
teaching myself,
one misstep after another.
Mom's next try at sex ed,
morning of my wedding
at nineteen. *Have you done
Anything about birth control?
You are short like me,
I got pregnant right away,
it took my twin sister,
two inches taller than me
two years to get pregnant.*

Velvet Tobacco

This stepping out into
what is unknown,
uncharted, and shaky -
that's called liberation.
　　　　　　—Pema Chödrön

I dream that my mother is smoking
a cigar in my bedroom before dawn.
The idea of her enjoying tobacco
wrapped in paper or leaf is unbelievable,
let-alone the notion of her inhaling smoke,
ludicrous by itself but puffing a cigar
early morning to wake me, her lost
daughter, is side-splittingly funny.
When dad rolled his own cigarettes
using tobacco from a red Velvet can,
she pinched her nose, turned away
because smoke bothered her. I try
to imagine my mother sitting outside
at a baseball game sipping whiskey
with a stogie dangling from her lips.
The picture cannot form in my awake
brain. She didn't even chew gum.
Out of bed and dressed, I sip fresh-
brewed coffee like my father did.
The notion of Mom joining Dad
for an after-breakfast smoke
rather than giving disapproving looks
is an idea to ponder. Would Dad
have loved Mom better if she'd shared
his vices? Would their marriage
have been happy, not the empty
shell it appeared to me.

Ham and Beans

My father planted with a two-row
planter and used a two-row picker
to harvest ears of corn,
stored the corn in corn cribs
with slatted air flow openings.

Autumn winds dried it better
then today's metal bin electric
dryers. When Dad was ready
to shell corn to grind or sell,
he called a contractor with a sheller,

then asked neighbors for help.
Ten to fifteen men answered his call,
carrying rakes and shovels to pull corn
toward the machine. The guys wore jeans
and overalls tucked into overshoes,

keeping mice and rats out of their pants
when the rakes exposed their dens,
leaving them for Raggs, the rat-terrier.
While Dad called the neighbors, Mom
prepared to feed those farmer friends.

She baked loaves of bread and pies -
three pies if harvest was large, likely
to last all day, cake for an afternoon break.
Early morning, she was up starting ham
hocks and beans in a pressure cooker.

Mom set me to work peeling potatoes
while she fed baby calves and chickens.
I peeled twenty pounds of spuds by ten a.m.,
mashed with loads of cream and butter,
served with ham and beans at noon.

Sour Cream Raisin

An old family standby
for holiday meals, the best
pie to take to picnics, pot-
luck dinners, and reunions.

My mom made extra filling
when baking pies, served us
sour cream raisin pudding,
as an after-country-school treat.

Her recipe is spare, with gaps
that must be filled with love
she never voiced. It assumes
homemade crust with lard rendered
from home-butchered hogs.

Recipe directs the cook
to boil the raisins but doesn't say
how many raisins
or how long to cook
or how much water to use,
always so much unsaid.

The sour cream was never
purchased in a store, cream
was skimmed after we milked
the Holsteins, left to sour
in the fridge.

Meringue in my memory's eye
was tall and perfectly browned,
prepared from free-range

hens' eggs, laid by chickens
she tended on the farm
along with the broilers she raised
and often served before pie.

Sour cream raisin pie
was never the same after my folks
retired and moved to town,
sold their chickens and pigs,
bought supplies from a store.

Bucket Calves

Another low pressure front
slated to bring icy sleet,
robs my sleep. I toss, turn,
count quilts.

Plenty of time to evoke visions
of Mom teaching baby Holsteins
to eat. She loved the newly
born, small enough to hold.

Straddling them, she cradled
calves' soft downy heads
against her aproned stomach,
inserted her fingers in babies'

mouths, dunking her hands
and calf's' noses in buckets
of warm cow's milk, pushing
against the little tongues

until they began to suck
her hand, taking in milk.
On the first or second try,
calves got it.

Rarely, there were three
or four new ones and I'd
be called on to hold buckets
while she taught the newest.

Week-old calves bunted
against their buckets, anxious
to eat, shoving me back
against wood panels.

Tilling

Years ago, when our son was one,
we moved out here to an acreage
on a quiet Wayne County road

surrounded by fallow fields, farmers yet
to begin spring planting. My folks came
to help us settle in. Dad brought his tiller,

carved a garden spot from this heavy clay.
With a reporter's eye I can see him dressed
in his soft grey hat, better, but not best

blue jeans, cuffed at the bottom
to have a handy place to fleck cigarette ashes,
a worn jean jacket over a blue work shirt,

red tobacco can, barely visible in his pocket.
He bent his back to the task of running
the tiller back and forth one way,

then a cross hatch to fluff the soil
soft enough for me to plant and his grandson
to play. After tilling he squatted on his heel,

used the other leg to balance, rolled a cigarette,
struck a match against those nearly new jeans,
lit it, inhaled, smiled

when the little tyke sat down in the dirt
beside him, pulled a snail from the soil,
showed it to his grandpa.

Plucked, Gutted, Singed

A box of baby chicks
arrived each spring, years
I was young, shipped

overnight from the hatchery.
Two hundred tiny balls
of yellow fluff, four hundred

pointy feet rushed from
a cramped box when opened
into a brooder house.

Dad installed a heat lamp
to warm the chicks
during cool May nights,

prevented chick pileups,
gave them a chance
to grow into laying hens

and broilers destined to be
fryers. I loved the little chicks,
but quickly grew tired of them.

They became old hens
bent on pecking my hands
gathering eggs.

The butchering debacle
kept me a safe distance away
as Mom snatched each

young broiler's feet
with a chicken hook.
She grasped both legs

in her left hand, placed
the head on an already
bloodied chopping block,

raised her right hand and axed.
The heads flew, quickly
snatched by Browser,

her big St. Bernard cross.
Each decapitated body
twitched, spewing blood

on her apron and across
anything or anyone close by.
After what seemed an eternity

of spurting blood, Mom
would add him to a growing
pile of future fried chicken

to be plucked, gutted, singed.
I still eat fried chicken, pretend
it's from heaven ready to fry.

Storm

Mother calls us to dinner by ringing that cursed bell
like warning of an impending tornado.

We sit down as a family to eat our noon meal,
as happy to be together as cats caged with Raggs, the rat terrier.

Del looks away, Wayne glares as if daring us to talk to him,
I stir my food, appetite gone.

Wearily, Dad says to Wayne, *please, pass the salt and pepper,*
Wayne stonewalls his father, arms crossed.

Dad yells this time,
> *Pass the Goddamn salt and pepper*
> *for Christ's sake.*

Wayne crosses his arms and glares at his father,
Dad grabs him by the arm and pushes him to the floor,

blames him for last night's rain on the cut alfalfa,
today's humidity spoiling the last chance to make hay,
his headache, and that God-awful bell.

Del and I flee, as if from a tsunami, food untouched,
falling over each other to get away.

Mother sits, lips clamped shut, eyes flashing like lightning.
Dad is no longer hungry, waits for the storm.

Yellowing Curtains

Dad stands in our tiny kitchen,
his five-foot-eight inches slumped
and tired, back to the blazing cob burner
warming his bones. He's already
in cap and ripped jacket,
dust pooling around his overshoes,
sipping one last cup of coffee
before morning chores.
He places the empty cup
on the enameled range behind
the cob stove, turns to leave when
Mom wraps her arms around his neck
to hug him. His now empty arms
hang limp at his sides, eyes
looking away and over her shoulder
toward the once-pretty yellow curtains
tucked behind the water heater.
Suddenly, no longer hungry
for my bowl of Grapenuts,
I look away too, not wanting
to see my mother's face.

Minced Ham Lunch

A day at my parent's farm in the 1960's began early with breakfast of
eggs
and toast or cereal followed by chores. After I married, I learned that
break-
fast included dessert at my in-law's. Breakfast there was bacon, eggs,
and toast
followed by a bowl of cereal, and a sweet roll. After we milked and
turned cows
out to pasture, fed baby calves, pigs, and chickens, Dad and my brothers
got haying equipment ready. Mom and I baked pies for dinner, and cake
or cookies for lunch. Dinner at noon was our main meal of the day.

While the oven was hot from baking, even on scorching days, Mom put
a roast
or a casserole in the oven for dinner. I was regularly assigned the job of
peeling
potatoes while Mom picked vegetables for our dinner. In the summer we
always
had mashed potatoes and gravy and seasonally worked our way through
new peas, green beans, carrots, beets, and finally a haying season's treat –
sweetcorn on-the-cob accompanied by just-picked sliced tomatoes.
Lunch was the snack between dinner at noon and evening supper or a
meal
kids ate at school. Mom made us minced ham sandwiches on white
bread
buttered with margarine for school lunches. She typically added cookies
or a piece of cake and apples in the fall but couldn't afford fruit out of
season.

After dinner when the dew was off the meadows the guys cut and raked
hay.
Mom and I did more dishes and got ready to deliver lunch to the hay
meadow
around three or four. She honed mid-afternoon lunch prep and field
delivery
to an art form. Occasionally, she took minced ham sandwiches to the

hayfield to serve before the sweets. Mom frosted chocolate cake with
      chocolate frosting
and cut it into large pieces or we packed dozens of chocolate chip
      cookies.
We loaded it in an oval metal tub she used to bathe us in when we were
      infants.

Mom filled the baby bathtub with plates, forks, and glasses. She made
      a big
pitcher of ice-tea loaded with ice to keep it cold. We packed everything
into the car. I rounded up my two younger brothers and Mom drove us
to the meadow, bumping along a rough track made by and for tractors.
We parked in a shady spot if the crew was near a shelterbelt or just on a
      flat.
The hay crew drove their tractors to us, happy to have a break in the
      shade,
even if just in the shade cast by the car. Ice-tea first, then sweets, washed
down with more tea. Half an hour later we would head back to the house
to start supper and bring cows in for milking. Hay crew quit for the
      day in time for chores.

.

Cooking with Love and Lard

Chicken fried in pork lard,
cream-cheese-mashed potatoes,
and green beans with bacon bits
like she always fixed for dad,
are poison to my daughter.
My explanation that her condition
abbreviated, PKU, is like a peanut
butter allergy was not helpful
to make Mom understand.
Protein doesn't cause choking
like peanuts can, but builds up, results
in brain damage, emotional wreckage.
Mother, who cooks with love, walks
away with tears in her eyes
at my stern words, when I, explain,
repeatedly that her granddaughter
cannot have protein and refuse to let
my girl eat her grandma's food.
Mom, not believing in this condition
she can't see, sneaks cheese curls
and chocolate bars to her youngest
granddaughter, believing that it won't
hurt Liz to have a bit. Even as a little
girl, my daughter knows how to say no.

Regret

I missed what turned out to be my last chance
to spend time with my father. Instead of talking
to him, I killed time cooking and cleaning
the year my folks were snowed-in here,
on our son's second birthday. Recovering
from daughter's C-section birth next spring,
I didn't visit him on Father's Day. Time
caught up with him in a life-altering stroke
that Holiday. It was followed by a year
of heart attacks and strokes. Heartbroken, I saw
him decline and finally lose his ability to speak.
We buried Dad on my son's next birthday.

Church Ladies

My folks were too busy for religion,
milked a few Holsteins, raised a few sows,
and butchered a few broilers
every summer until they retired.

After a farm sale they moved to town.
Mom was bored just keeping house,
volunteered for every church duty
from cleaning to planting flowers

to funeral meals, until Dad got sick.
Mom, like other post-WWII stay-at-home
wives, were backbones of their churches
until they became too old or disabled.

Weed-filled church flower beds were planted
to grass, Congregations hired janitors,
and interment meals are now catered.
It's been over forty years since Dad passed

and twenty since Mom joined him
but some things don't change in little hamlets
dotting Nebraska, like my adopted town,
a twin to the one near my parents' farm.

I received a We-Miss-You postcard
from the Methodist Church, inviting me
to a Hawaiian potluck, complete with guilt note
"Hope you can come," handwritten in a corner,

like pleas from mom when she lost her mobility,
felt neglected and called her children to fill her days.

A hospitality committee of retired ladies
dress in flowered costumes, greet the faithful

and the reluctant like me, with cheerful Alohas,
drape pink, blue and green leis around our necks,
invite us to enjoy supper, tell us, *Thanks
for coming,* as we leave.

Mom would have loved potluck.

Iris Garden

Mom presented her well-tended
Iris garden each spring. Bearded beauties
marched along sidewalks, grinned
amid barberry thorns, leaned
against the brick foundation, escorted
visitors to her front door.
She sought hybrids to express
moods she couldn't describe,
Night Ruler's black struck a somber
note, Play With Fire's scarlet
spoke to her inner beauty,
Monet's Blue took her to twilights
back on the farm, Orange Harvest invited
smiles, English Charm's delicate petals
barely visible in the morning sun.

I admired the flowers to please her
more than for their beauty.
She and they seemed timeless
until she couldn't weed,
prune, water as needed,
started to give them away.
Neighbors invited to take bulbs
when she moved to assisted living.
Those left behind stayed
to bloom another year until
erased by the new owner 's mower.

Naked Ladies

Lush green naked lady leaves appear early April
pushing through soil in crowded blade clumps.

They stretch their legs, grow through
snow and cold rain.

Never easy with calling a flower *naked*,
Mom called them surprise lilies.

Their leaves are short-lived, browning
in May, gone by June, her birth month.

They share space with giant tiger lilies
and floppy poppies in July garden's real estate.

Naked, slender green stalks emerge in August.
The flower's rocket-powered energy shoots

skyward, pale pink lilies surprise us with golden
stamens, fuzzy pistols aimed at the sun.

Asters follow, covering ladies' bare bottoms.
Towering lavender asters shout,

Look at me. In September,
ladies fold up shop for the year.

Angels

Mother told anyone who would listen, she saw angels
hovering near the ceiling. Dressed in white, the spirits
flew above her hospital bed and distracted her
from cancer's pain. Immobilized in piles of snowy cotton
bedding, she asked me to pluck her chin whiskers
and directed me to look in the room's corners, willing me
to see her cherubs. They visited her when no one was there;
shy creatures destined just for her, but she wanted me to see

her precious winged visions. The oldest son came every day,
took care of the details; second son came only near the end;
third son too stressed to face her death wouldn't enter
the sick room; fourth son traveled a distance when he could;
and I, the only daughter, visited in between, helped her feel
pretty, and witnessed her lucidity fly away with the angels.

If the Shoe Fits

Driving last evening, I saw one lone Crocs
on the side of the cemetery road
as if someone took a big step out of it
and forgot to go back
or they were being chased and lost
their footwear during pursuit.

Belongings get lost,

like my assortment of lone earrings.
With no notion of how or when their mates
went missing I've checked under car seats,
dressers, and in dusty rarely worn boots.

No earrings.

People get lost too, like my oldest brother
at five who hid in a tree for hours watching
searchers. Or my younger brother at fifty-five
who moved away from his notion of family
and is still gone. Would I know him if I saw him
by the side of the road after all these years?

Slippers

Furnace runs almost non-stop.
I wear my mother's old slippers
first thing in the morning,
before bed at night
warming my feet in her memory.

II.

Mother, May I

Prostitutes and destitutes
And temptresses like me
— Joni Mitchell, *The Magdalene Laundries*

date a Catholic boy?
Question asked and answered
with an emphatic *No*
from my mother
raised conservative Christian.
Mom married a close-mouthed
non-practicing Methodist
who didn't know how to show love.
She grieved her sister's seduction by
and marriage to a Catholic man.
I was, if not quite innocent, at least chaste,
pretty in my own way, but she saw me
as a temptress luring the wrong kind of men.
She was unhappy I married a Lutheran.
What would she say if she was alive today
to learn the Lutheran didn't work out,
just like she predicted
and I'm dating a divorced Catholic?
My uncle was adopted from a prostitute
Mom said, although no one
knows for sure. His past was murky,
his adopted family nearly destitute.
He fathered three girls – molested
the middle one so the story goes,
his acts ruining her life.
He never had much growing up,
never said, *Mother, may I,*
just took what he wanted.

I Try to Picture Mom

Be as scarlet as you like
                    —Marjorie Saiser

with a checkered past.
She was raised like a Puritan
in a tight-fisted Scottish household.
I remember her as a woman
who stitched her bra tips down
to avoid even a hint of nipples,
a woman without indoor plumbing
who took spit baths with a washcloth
in teakettle-heated well water
behind her bedroom door, a woman
who worried endlessly about my modesty,
admonishing me repeatedly -
Do not get pregnant in high school.
She never touched alcohol,
looked down at those who imbibed,
giggled like a teenage girl at my wedding
when unbeknownst to her
the punch was spiked.

Mom could have hit the bars
while Dad was away at war,
sung Billy Holiday songs in Blues Clubs,
hung out with other girls in high heels
and tight dresses flirting with sailors,
but it's hard to imagine.

Letter to My Sixteen-year-old Self

Hey kid, be patient, don't run away,
you'll be old enough to leave home
pretty soon; finish high school.
Figure out your future.

Don't fool yourself, you're too immature
to run away. You don't have a clue
how to take care of yourself, never
held a job, not even volunteer work.

Bury your head in books, try to be polite
to your family. They are doing as well
as possible given their limited income,
attitudes, old-fashioned ideas.

Talk to your dad more. He was thoughtful
but didn't know how to communicate
with his wife and daughter. He did fine
chatting with his sons or other men.

Don't be intimidated when your mother
threatens, *wait till your father gets home.*
Try to understand Dad didn't want to deal
with kid's misbehavior after long days in the field.

Caution your brothers to let go of stubbornness
like refusing to pass the pepper to Dad
when he's hungry; step up and protect
them from resulting blows.

Hey kid, speak up for yourself, be obnoxious
occasionally; don't go through life silently
angry at your mom for not protecting her children,
guilty when Dad's anger passed you, visited a brother.

Middle Child

My father is buried less than two hundred meters from where we sit now. I walk out there often, and I talk to him. I talk to him as I could never do in life.
—Cormac McCarthy, *All the Pretty Horses*

My handsome Dad was jilted twice in the late 1930's, done with women so
     the tale is told,
he signed up to serve his country.

He did not believe women should enlist, called them "harlets," but
     changed his mind about love
when he met Mom.

She wanted to serve her country too, but stayed home to please him,
got a job building bombs.

He shipped out to India. Their caste system bolstered his notion women
are either devils or angels.

Dad called me Sister, his only daughter, as if he didn't remember the name
    he chose
for me sandwiched between his four sons.

Lost as a teen, I aped other's war politics till my father with his war
     memories, corrected me,
teaching lessons of peace.

Stung by his criticism, I walked gravel roads and sand pastures alone
in search of a clear path.

Today I visit his grave, ask my father about the big questions I was not
    brave enough
to do when he was alive.

Cat Lady

There is no gate, no lock, no bolt that you can set upon the freedom of my mind.
                                          —Virginia Woolf

I am the old lady with too many cats,
unwilling to tie them in a gunny sack
to drown them like my mother did.

She trashed baby kittens like a soldier
killed during war. In xenophobic
frenzy she destroyed if she didn't like

kitten's type or color, selectively
breeding for yellow and white.
I suppose she had money woes

and other life complications but it broke
my eight-year-old heart when I saw
her dunk a sack of mewing babies

in the cattle tank. She held them down,
until all the crying and struggling ended.
It wasn't the first or last time she played

out this drama with little lives. Yet,
later in life she kept one sickly calico
house cat well into both their old ages.

Progeny

I'm suddenly tired, never been this tired of this question that's always asked if you're a woman.
—Susan Browne, *Do you have children?*

Both grandmothers
died when I was too young
to remember them,
and I have no sense of their place.
I always get questions
when I meet someone
my age or older,
and often now
from anyone over fifty,
Do you have grandchildren? or
How many grandchildren do you have?
And from those who just assume
everyone has them,
How old are your grandkids?
When I answer in the negative
and joke about grand-dogs,
the next comment
is always, *I'm so sorry,*
as if I should be pitied
for having children
who have not reproduced. I can
only imagine the pressure
my daughter and daughter-in-law
feel with society's incessant pushing.
As if raising offspring is a woman's
only useful contribution.

Grandmother's Gifts

Mom took me to see her mother
as Granny lay dying when I was six,
doing a daughterly duty like a mother
robin feeding worms to her young.

I asked Mom to talk about her mother
when I was old enough to want to know
but Mom clammed up like an old door
warped shut. From family stories,

I learned maternal gran loved books, taught
in a one-room school until she wed in 1914.
Mom oft said her glass-fronted secretary,
should be for dishes, and ditched Gran's books.

Paternal grandma perished when I
was a wee girl. Dad's father summered
with us for years after she passed in a silver
travel trailer brightly lit like a Roma caravan.

Grandpa gave me Grandma's porcelain doll
rather than to his grown daughters believing
dollies are for little girls to play make believe
and I imagined her playing with me.

Dad's mother was a seamstress who taught him
to sew. He in turn taught Mom to patch his jeans.
I learned in 4H, got an electric iron, donated
Granny's twenty-pound pressing iron to a museum.

Maternal Grand's secretary now sits
in my dining room full of seldom used China.

Books fill shelves, tables, and nightstands
like Mom and her mother are wresting for control.

The porcelain doll from my paternal granny
rests in her box waiting to be passed
on to another little one rather than sitting
in a museum or unused like my dishes.

Neighborhood

I walked alone to visit neighbors'
farms in the '60's, delivering eggs
or buying groceries.

Myrtle and Maisie, a mile west,
fussed over me,
fed me cookies and iced tea.

Rarely, I walked past their farmstead
another mile to St. John's Church,
then one more mile to Kelly's place
for bread or cheerios.

St. John vicarage's lawn was full of crosses,
fountains and statues of the Virgin Mary.
I yearned for yard art besides hollyhocks
and daisies in our very Methodist yard.

The church bell tower rose above
all but the highest cottonwoods.
Bells announcing daily mass
were heard for miles on still mornings.

Mrs. Kelly, faithful to the Church's
teaching birthed a dozen children,
the last born, the year she died.

The family sold chemical fertilizer
but never linked it to her cancer.

Hunting for birds, one of their older boys
killed his younger brother, who popped out

of a car door in front of his brother's gun,
like a jack-in-the-box gone wrong.

Their mother already gone that year,
family grieved anew. St. John's bells
tolled for funeral mass, again.

Interchangeable

Twelve, breasts budding, I was
mystified by my changing body,
waking in the mornings, different,
like an alien invaded during sleep.

Boys who never paid attention before,
wanted to unsnap my bra, touch
my tender nipples,
slip hands into my panties.

At thirteen, I believed guys liked me
for me, by fifteen, I realized boys
just wanted to touch
and girls were interchangeable.

I walked along the creek,
down a sand road to Jo's house,
away from family,
pretending I was someone else.

I lacked courage to tell them all
to "fuck-off." too shy to swear
out loud back then. I make up for
that reluctance today.

Brains in Our Knees

Follow your Inner moonlight; don't hide the madness.
—Allen Ginsberg

Days at the end of November are as short
as my rolled-up high school skirts

Thanksgiving feasts without pie
are like hot cocoa without chocolate

Sleeping dogs are like slumbering rattlers,
shaking dangerous tails when suddenly roused

Horses without riders are the waters
Moses parted, only momentarily tamed

Failing to think outside the box is a trap
my bosses use to fire people

I always ask what or where the box was
and why we need to think outside it

and questioned my high school math teacher -
why do one and one equal two?

He rolled his eyes like they were inked rollers
ready to print a newspaper, headlined

I can't teach girls who wear short skirts like our brains
were in our knees or his was between his legs

Night falls quickly at Thanksgiving
like my rolled-down waistbands before home

Go West

September is a time of breaking rules
in high school,
away-game football,
pep club buses packed wall-to-wall
with thirty or more members
singing, *See you in September,*
off-key screaming,
California Dreaming.
Songs' siren calls aroused
but I lacked courage to run away. I vowed
to leave milk cows
behind and go west with flair,
wear flowers in my hair.
Never made it there,
went east,
where even the least
of the well-to-do fly high
like Holden in *Catcher in the Rye,*
attend prep school
paid for by rich parents vacationing in Istanbul.
Bought my own bus, a cool
VW Microbus one September
and pretended.

Out of Body

> *...Well, when I woke up*
> *The rain was pourin' down*
> *There were people standing all around...*
> —J. Frank Wilson

Close my eyes, and I'm back there,
scarlet blood flows
        from slashed skin wounds,
ruby bubbles blow
        from one victim's nose,
crimson droplets seep
        from another's mouth,
a child's cheeks changes
        from ruby to purple-blue,

I hear, *Where oh where can my baby be,*
pass out on the shop class cement floor,
hit my head a good whack, I'm told.

My classmates watch the rest of a car
crash movie where all the victims
tell the audience the blood is fake.

The janitor carries me to his storeroom office;
shop teacher and students crowd his door
to watch like window shoppers at Christmas.

I hover near the ceiling,
        watch them look at my body,
wonder why they're making such a fuss.
Wish they would quit shaking
        my shoulder to wake me

I Feel Sorry for the Other Mothers

Mom grew up in the nineteen-thirties,
dreamed of being a beautician

but had to work as a live-in housekeeper
during high school to pay her way,

further study out of reach
in a time, desires went unrealized.

I was named high school valedictorian,
received scholarships. Mother didn't say,
Congratulations.

She said, *"I'm sorry for the other mothers.
They didn't hear their kids' names called."*

She was more disappointed when I signed up
to study psychology at a university

telling her I wanted to help others - in truth
it was to understand my family.

Remorse

Our ultimate freedom is the right and power to decide
how anybody or anything outside ourselves will affect us.
—Stephen Covey

I was so easily flattered
it's embarrassing. This need
to be admired transcended
everything then. He worked
there when I began my first
job after graduate school,
ten years older, slow smile,
soft brown eyes, come-hither
looks. Same expression
as that time back when I
was a freshman in college,
where an older grad student
targeted me with same come-to-me
look in his exotic brown eyes.
I knew little of predators,
less still of men from other
countries, didn't understand
grooming. I fell for the wink-
nod-keep-this-our-secret idea,
didn't know how to explain
to my, we-married-too-young
husband, about the baffling-
to-me-gifts, the silver belt,
the red sari. I didn't even
know how to say fuck-off
then because I did not use
that kind of language.
I carry this stone with me,
offer help to others
as my way to atone.

Cherry Pie For Breakfast

The wife wants to reconcile
with her estranged man.
She bares her soul
in a letter of contrition
and vulnerability,
admitting her faults.

She bakes a cherry pie
from cherries she hand-picked
last summer,
leaves it for him
with the letter,
hopeful that it will
pry open a tiny corner
of his walled-off heart.

The husband leaves a *thank you*
note confessing his love,
makes a first apology
for his contribution
to the marital mess.
The letter is careful
not to make commitments
or to express intentions.

She finds a message left
on their computer, sent
to his lover, merrily stating,
cherry pie for breakfast,
dated and timed twenty minutes
after he finds the pie.

Home Early or Not at All

I wasn't meant for waiting
and wondering, Gus, she said.
—Larry McMurtry

He'll be home early or not at all
It's Saturday night, time to howl
Squealing tires on his tired El Camino
He flees the domestic scene – oh.
She goes to find a friendly face
at Smoky Samz, the local bar,
wants to improve the night's pace
but hasn't done well alone so far.
Another meal at the kitchen table
strikes her as one more fable
sold to women to keep them happy
while their men treat them crappy.
He returns somber and contrite.
She stays out all the next night,
puts on a brave new morning face,
knows it's time for a safer place.

Epigenetics

Pregnant with my daughter
I drove highways and dirt roads
often drifted nearly shut,
bitter, snowy winter of '84,
lugged my almost three-year old son
into, then out of, a car seat
each morning for his day at the sitter
while I counseled other people's kids.

I've wondered
about the nature of nurture,
since my daughter was born
that year with PKU, an inherited
condition; one recessive gene
from her father, other one from me,
Type I Diabetes diagnosed
six years later, Thyroid deficiency
in her twenties, and another
autoimmune condition,
Celiac, five years later,

I've stewed over the strain
of the pregnancy year and chance
it contributed to her challenges,
comforting myself or perhaps
lying to myself there was nothing I did
to compromise her immunity,
nothing could have stopped recessive genes
meeting, colliding, expressing.

I'm staring mother-guilt
in the face again as the science

of epigenetics tells the story
of changes in a generation,
how in-utero effects formed her
and will alter her unborn,
should she decide to conceive,
my stress, her trauma,
destined for future generations.

Once a bridesmaid

I was a bridesmaid only once
when I was 22, three years married,
bride 25. We met when she volunteered
at the group home my husband and I
managed for six teen-age boys shifting
from Syracuse Developmental Center
to the community. She was a calm,
comforting person for the boisterous boys,
like a feather pillow at the end of a hectic
day. Occasionally she brought along
her boyfriend, unflappable to boy's
hijinks. Bride-to-be and fiancé lived
like monks for a long year before
the wedding; her Jewish, his Catholic
values clashing over trifles.
I was honored to stand by her side
in his parent's crowded house
as they said their vows under joint
direction of a priest and a rabbi.
The wedding party traveled
to a sprawling apartment to party
under her mom's watchful eyes.
They served Polish sausage and unleavened
bread lovingly prepared by both families.
Their marriage was a smashing success,
four daughters and a long life together
until his early death. Married young,
my husband and I hailed from protestant
Nebraska farm families, me half-baked
Methodist, he from a family of devout
Lutherans. We mixed white flour
and white flour to make uneatable bread.

Cranberry Mornings

Old calico cat in summer
lived a bibliography
of scratching - trees,
board fences, deck railing,
came inside to sleep content,
like a baby fresh from suckling.
I read the same catalog,
spent long hours outside,
soaking in those exquisite rays,
slept like a proverbial dog.

Confronted by late Autumn's
sudden cold, frigid winds,
cloudy days, she goes to the door,
bamboozles me, turns back.
My bloodlust flashes when I
catch her scratching
my leather couch, issue stern
words, warn her I'll send
her to perdition, then
provide a scratching log.
I too, go outside only as needed
these cranberry mornings,
a living contradiction
to my stern admonitions.

Cigars in the Back Yard

Quiet by the firepit
in the middle of a medium-size town
reminds of a time alone in a hotel
in another medium-size berg,
awake in the wee hours,
listening to coal trains whistle their lonesome song,
hauling loads from Wyoming
going east to feed coal-fired power plants.
Citizens alarmed about greenhouse gases overheating
Earth, are pushing to phase out coal,
replace with solar panels
like the solar field on the other side of town
and wind farms like the hundreds of turbines
in my county.

She lights a cigar,
scatters bird seed,
savors the calm moment.
I congratulate her on her new book.
We discuss mothering daughters,
daughtering mothers,
sip cabernet,
warm our hands over the wood fire,
on an unseasonably cool day,
chat about success of the festival,
wait for birds to flock to her feeder,
talk about growing fruit trees,
plan next summer's wine.

Sweet Warmth

My mom's fingers were long
and thin, but in my memory's eye
the blue-lined pattern sketched

across hers is the same design
as the one that zigzags
across mine. Blue veins

on my pale hands pop up
like frogs from a mucky
pond as I peel new potatoes,

watch a blood-red September
sunrise draw a horizontal line
across the sky heralding

summer's end. Labor Day
has a melancholy drift,
often gifting me with the blues.

It is the beginning of school,
the best daytime hours indoors.
Rising early to drive kids and me

to classes, we miss September's
last blaze of sweet warmth.
School's finally out for all of us.

I'll ignore my aging hands, revel
in beautiful fall mornings.
A friend planning to retire soon

looks forward to cigars
and whisky after dinner,
cradled in blue-lined hands.

Grave Site

What Goes Around, Comes around
—Waylon Jennings

Family graves are scattered
like dandelion fluff in a strong wind
across boneyards along Highway 275.

I attend one of the veterans' programs
on Memorial Day and meet old friends.

Together we are a color wheel - one is a faded
blonde, and another's hair is still red,
mine gone white this year.

They tell the tale of my classmate's ashes
claimed by his ex-wife who keeps them
on top of her refrigerator.

Blonde sister's angry and searching for a way
to reclaim their brother.

Another story floats on the flag-lifting breeze
of a man who loved many women.

Memorial service brings the third wife
and last girlfriend
face-to-face over his headstone.

Cemetery is located a mile
from my parent's first farm. Pandemic
inspired me to buy a plot there.

My future grave site has clear sight
of that farm's hilly pasture.

After a lifelong struggle to separate from family
my future grave is yards away
from my parent's headstone.

Their bones, my ashes,
resting together in perpetuity

Flying Dream

Everyone dreams of flying
they say, yet my recent dream

of flying is the first one I recall
in my sixty-plus years.

Beating my wings against
the twin conventions

of parenting small children
and meeting boss's demands

has kept me grounded.
Finally free, I skim over treetops

like a redtail floating on warm
up-drafts, meet geese flying

in great V's, white feathers
as brilliant against morning's

crystal azure sky as a white
cat's sapphire eyes stand out

from his silvery fur.
Two years after planned,

I fly to Ireland to spend time
with a friend's family honoring

her winged life before cancer.
I close my eyes and dream

of gliding like geese and hawks,
                    carefree.

Crimson

Some days, time is a lazy river
meandering through
greening pastures, warm
sunshine after summer rain,
watching kittens' tumble.

It's a vase of yellow roses
delivered to your door,
a friend's surprise visit,
seeing red-gold dawns.

Rarely, days are cobwebs;
ready to tuck kitties safely
in the shed, you slip
and you are down, head
striking edge of a sidewalk.

Consciousness socketed,
when you wake and search
for the hurt place, fingertips
red, white hair drips crimson.

Other days are middling,
You sleep in spurts, headaches
come and go, lump on your head
for days is finally gone.

Then, you find most days
are just days, you wake,
say hello to another morning,
pour a cup of coffee.

Wild Yellow Rose

No scent is sweeter
than the wild yellow rose,
its wicked brambles,
those fragile flowers.

They bloom for a day or two,
reliably in May. When one dies
another opens to fill the void,
spent petals blow in the wind.

A bush grew in my folk's yard
by one end of Mom's clothesline.
Only hang the jeans, old towels
on the line by the roses, she said.

I took a cutting,
planted it in my own yard
the summer before
my parent's farm sale.

Loving the scent of this rose
and its delicate flower, I
carried yellow roses
on my wedding day.

My daughter's nuptial bouquet
contained yellow roses too;
I pray her marriage endures
like a fine cabernet.

Pruned often in forty years
it has bloomed here, I place

roses on my parent's graves
each Memorial Day.

Blossoms each year are
frailer, fleeting,
marking life's passing.

III.

Ode to the Letter E

I have empathy for you E, evicted from alphabet's
top, an A with your side eviscerated and elongated,
evermore in fifth place. You are now elegant emerald
earrings, eggs, endives, and eggplants.

As our eyes and ears, you stand tall for education,
emaciated prisoners, enthralled youth, essential
care for the elderly, homeless emigrants,
and those with elemental eating disorders.

E, you are the elephant in the room during elections.
You are Prophet Ezekiel, Emily Dickinson, Elvis. You
embody daughter Elizabeth's efforts, son Ezechiel's energy.

You elevate my entire being with ease, your electric
presence emits effervescence like an extra dose of fizz
in an elderberry soda, energizes with scent of evergreen.

Unwanted Beauty

We rarely see beauty in ourselves
but occasionally someone sees it in us.
In nature, Canada, bull, and musk
thistles are unwanted beauties.
They are declared noxious by Weed Boards
that look over fields, send landowners
warning notices to clean up, and if weeds
are not removed on time, levy big fines.
Thistles produce lovely purple flowers
that mature into fluff-covered ripe seeds.
One must snip carefully, pile cottony
seed heads together in a bag and remove
before they blow with summer's
furnace winds across vast grasslands,
dispersing noxious weed seeds
viable for fifty years. It's my fervent hope
we clear our personal toxic weeds.
Plant seeds of change, feel the beauty
that's been there all along.

Clover's Flowers

My daughter's loveliness
shines like a beacon from afar
calling us to be less slovenly
in our ways.
She skips through meadows
of clover flowers at dawn.
Honeybees follow her trips
like hot tea goes along
with gingerbread.
The sweet scent draws
cloven-hoofed beasts
and forlorn lovers
to linger with her
in gold-colored pullovers.

Tin Lizzie

Son's recent birthday reminded me of his and his sister's
preschool years. Memories reached out and grabbed me
from my dreams, demanded I rise to record the highs
and lows. Kids had a series of sitters: Debbie, Connie,
Carolyn, Lydia, who gently saw them through their toddler
and pre-school years while their father and I built careers.

Liz was in tears after her first day at Carolyn's
make-shift daycare. Her husband teased everyone - Liz
about her name. It reminded him of a Model T, so called
by people watching a 1922 car race. One of the cars
named Liz, was in such bad shape it looked like a painted
tin can. After that Model Ts became known as Tin Lizzies.

Liz was diagnosed with PKU at birth, started on special
formula at two weeks old. This started our education.
We in turn educated every daycare provider and sitter.
Most could not believe she could not have meat, cheese,
or eggs or that vegetables have measurable protein.
Liz's fifth birthday found us at Kindergarten Roundup
explaining to the school about diet requirements.

Everything got more complicated the first-grade spring
when Liz was diagnosed again, another step
in her autoimmune system breakdown, more diet limitations,
preparing her for years ahead of thyroid disfunction,
Celiac, and iron infusions for anemia from her limited diet.
No one calls her Tin Lizzie now; we call her incredibly brave.

Community Spread

Scraping paint from a shed,
I strip away virus fear with paint chips,
hurrying to finish while October

sun warms my face. Painting
soaks me in vitamin D,
strengthens my immunity.

My sister-in-law's brother
is dead at sixty after contracting
Covid at a wedding.

Sick college students are sent
to hotels to recover on an honor
system to stay there

but like prisoners on work release
can't resist temptation to escape.
They get meals delivered weekdays,

go home weekends, spread germs
to family, return to the hotel,
hope no one notices,

check in with a nurse, return
to dorm and classes. Faculty
daily confront risk

of teaching reckless freshmen,
change clothes and shower
as soon as they go home

fearing they'll carry virus to family
like Liz, immune-compromised.

People celebrate with big weddings,
but hold private graveside goodbyes
like family's brother, this week.

I have tea with Liz on her porch.
We soak in vitamin D like our lives
depend on it because they may.

Nerves

*Art is a language which anneals individuals to each other
through experiences that are uniquely human.*
—Ann Lauterbach

Nervous disorders are often passed
from one generation to the next.
Mom called her headaches and nausea
nervous headaches.

Mom gossiped about family, without thought,
slandering kin of one of her daughters-in-law.
Dad got involved, offered to shoulder a shotgun.
County sheriff cautioned them about threats.

My older brothers and I confronted her
about those evil words. Not able to face us,
she collapsed in the yard. I ignored her tantrum.
My husband helped her stand.
.

Mom's brother had a tick in his left eye
when he was upset or stressed. He was so attached
to his father, he died at forty-eight from stress
of losing his elderly dad two weeks prior.

When I landed in the hospital as a teenager
after a bout of tremors; exhausted, too busy to eat,
the doctor, knowing our family history,
called it *nerves*, fed me, and sent me home.

I ingest Tylenol to quiet pain from cracked feet,
dry skin scratching that wakes me from a sound sleep.
Jan, friend and confident, before she died from cancer,

believed a person will have disease in places that itch.

I po-pawed the idea at the time believing it artistic
affectation but now the idea sits with me,
like a prediction of doom, stokes my fear of dying
from tumors like Mom and her twin sister did.

My daughter has a potpourri of conditions
causing nausea, diarrhea, and headache.
Together they are labeled *anxiety.* Today's
Zoloft and Prozac help her, and others cope.

My Mother, My Daughter

*Aging is an extraordinary process whereby you become
the person that you always should have been.*
—David Bowie

I could not wait to leave home
summer after high school,
rented a room from a family

that didn't even like me, just
glad to escape Mom's gossip
about her neighbors.

At twenty-five, I lived
five states from home,
tried to pretend I was adopted.

My daughter at twenty-five
Is delightful, we see a Harry
Potter movie together,

whisper through the previews,
quiet as the scene opens,
cry at the same parts,

startle together
as the action changes.

Quiet until after the flick,
then a flood of comments,
remarks about parts

we really liked,

how well the movie
followed the book or didn't.

My daughter's birth
mended rifts, real
and imagined with my mom

as they seemed to me
cut from the same cloth,
no guile, no pretense.

Birthday Storms

Liz was born in 1984 on a rainy March Day
after record snowfall that winter, spring-melt
back roads mired in mud. In 2018 we celebrate

her 34th with front yard cocktails
in sixty-degree sunshine, her 35th in 2019
with a raging storm-cyclone, two-plus inches

of rain, and widespread flooding in three states.
Her ailing retriever Roxie, storm-terrified
wrapped often in a thunder-shirt, old

Irish setter Monk scared-stiff by thunder
hid in the bathtub like a piece of art.
In 2020, Liz 's 36th coincided

with a highly contagious coronavirus
that infected people around the world.
Virus fear, given her medical vulnerability,

confined her at home, changed the way
we all lived and worked. Liz's 2020's seclusion
was only bearable by her private outdoor wedding,

and Gatsby, a Great Pyrenees-mix puppy.
Her 37th in 2021 occurred as vaccines
were offered and as a massive blizzard

in the Rockies swept east, spewed tornados
south to Texas, dropped trees, knocked out power.
Birthday gatherings cancelled again.

She celebrated with cocktails indoors
by candlelight with her soulmate,
enormous year-old Gatsby at their side.

When Tulips Bloom

My nine-year-old son quipped, *flu's going around school*
to explain his sister's illness. This six-year-old kindergartener
is sick. Born unable to cope with meat, eggs, or cheese.

She's thin as a starved calf. Not hungry or thirsty,
runs a fever and only wants to sleep.
It's early spring when the daffodils bloom.

I take her to the doc to insure it's not another immune system
issue and just the flu this time.
The clinic nurse can't raise a vein, refers us on.

She barely fusses, leans her head on my chest like a wilted flower.
Our local hospital sends her by ambulance to a city ER,
nurses place pressure, warm compresses on her femur artery.

My baby screams, *stop standing on my leg*. A diagnosis
of Type I Diabetes, and magic of insulin brings her around,
but she refuses the protein drink that sustains her brain.

Endocrinologists confer with dietitians and physicians.
They hunch together like buzzards over roadkill, and give her
an ultimatum, *drink your formula or we'll have to do it for you.*

This six-year-old clamps her mouth shut like she has lockjaw;
we cajole her to no avail, the doctor sighs, issues the order,
Insert the feeding tube. We watch. She screams. Tube is pushed

up her nose, down her throat into her stomach. The nurse slowly
pours formula through a funnel like she's filling her thermos with
      coffee.
The tube slides back out easily like's it's greased with butter.

Crying, our little girl turns her back on us, as if to say,
Why didn't you help me? Next day, her doctor offers a choice,
Drink or we'll use the tube again. She reluctantly begins to sip,

formula restoring body and spirit. Discharge after a week,
adjusting to insulin, her rosy cheeks as colorful
as the red and pink tulips blooming at home.

Victims

During a long cold winter
we applied for a wild game permit,
mailed-ordered wild turkey
hatchlings like we were buying
dishes from a JC Penney catalog.
Tiny fuzzy babies shipped
overnight from a hatchery,
arrived hungry but healthy.
We posted No Hunting signs,
started them in a corncrib home.
They quickly grew bronze-
green feathers, learned to fly,
outgrew the crib, roosted
in trees, on building peaks,
and often sat on deck railings.
They pecked at glass doors
like guests ringing a doorbell.
In fall we watched toms' fan
their tail feathers, strut in elaborate
courtship displays to impress
hens indifferent to their antics,
like teen boys perform skateboard
tricks to show off to young girls.
Early one morning I heard
our two-year-old daughter
scream, rushed to find her
surrounded by eight 25-pound
turkeys ready to peck her head,
like bullies harassing a victim.
They scattered at my call,
regrouped to chase barn cats
that readily eluded them.

The flock developed a circuit
around the grove, then further
afield out of our No Hunting
protection, searching for insects
or wild kin. Fewer returned
each trip until none were left,
except in Liz's memory,
victim to coyote attacks, vehicle
accidents, and hunting season.

Seedlings

Liz tried to ignore illness in those early years.
She and her big brother helped plant woodlot trees
every spring for ten years, hundreds of trees -

ponderosa, jack pine, red cedar, and locust. Trees
to shelter our home; old trees, cut, split in pieces to feed
the woodstove. We regret planting self-seeding cedar

and locust, still chop those seedlings every summer.
Born with PKU, another condition grew unchecked,
Type I Diabetes arrived like an invasive species at six.

One spring we planted one hundred oaks, surrounded
seedlings with weed mats, stapled them to the ground,
topped with tomato cages to protect the seedlings.

None lived. The heavy yellow clay cannot feed an oak
any more than Liz's system can fight diseases. She learned
to give herself shots, we learned to grow fruits and veggies.

We planted a handful of baby trees north of house and barns,
building a windbreak against relentless winter gales.
Trees flourished as Liz grew. Our son shot up tall,

rarely sick, outpaced trees' progress, learned to run a saw.
Tree branches too close to buildings needed pruning.
Their father cut; I hauled branches.

One small tree came down. We moved to another.
Liz wrapped her arms around that tree's trunk, desperate
to control this one thing in her world. *If I were in the way*

she tearfully screamed at us; *I suppose you'd just cut me down too.*

She Won a Purple Ribbon

She rode Rosie
when she was eight
and in love with animals,
accompanied her dad and brother horseback
to check cattle a mile away
in a pasture next to a friend's house
on a cool autumn Saturday,
returned home with a tiny grey-and-white
seal-point Siamese kitty born in the friend's barn
from a stray mouse-grey barn-cat mother
and an unknown father;
kitten tucked inside her zipped-to-the chin jacket
held in place with one hand
while gripping Rosie's reins with the other.
My girl adopted and raised
the kitty as a baby,
named him Smoky
to match the color of his fur
and entered
him in the county fair
the next summer, so well trained
he didn't need to be restrained.
She showed him without a leash
and won a purple ribbon
for Best Cat in her age bracket.

Chop Suey

Trauma is not just an event that took place sometime in the past;
it is also the imprint left by that experience on mind, brain, and body.
—Bessel Van der Kolk, MD

My daughter wrote lists
in a math notebook
during high school
but not math equations.
Chop suey, prominent
on multiple entries,
conjures foods
from her numerous diet
restrictions - some present
during those years,
foreshadowing others
waiting in the wings
to snag her as an adult,
stealthily, like red-tailed hawks
stalk rabbits.

From birth, no meat, no eggs,
age six, no sugar.
She wrote about sibling rivalry,
importance of education,
lava lamps,
sandwiched between
house floorplans,
song titles, and colored graphics.
The chop suey of ideas,
in her discarded notebook
sustained her imagination,
prepared her for an
unknowable time ahead,

in her thirties, no gluten,
and mental health challenges
of managing it all.

Dressing Vegetables

Cooking is a culinary art
like painting and sculpture.
To cook low protein, chef must
avoid meat, cheese, and eggs,
consult a reference list as even
vegetables differ in proteins;
potatoes, corn, and peas
on the high end of daily protein
counts – beets, lettuce, carrots
on the lower part of the scale.
Sweets were ok for my daughter
until she contracted Type I
Diabetes during kindergarten.
I cooked, adjusting ingredients
to maintain each new diet.

Gib is a gourmet cook
specializing in Indian curries,
chocolate mousse, and triple-
chocolate cake with fudge frosting.
He prefers vegetarian food,
grows tomatoes and basil,
visits farmer's markets for more,
cooks vegetarian chilies, stuffing,
and rice casseroles all liberally
spiced with garlic and peppers,
serves two or three sambals
at every dinner. He invites a cadre
of friends; his table a place
of comradery, spirited talk,
and laughter.

I learned to make beet curry,
garlic roasted carrots, and to
include fruits, kale, cabbage,
new lettuce varieties in salads.

Primary

I dream of tulips,
green grass covering Lincoln
neighborhoods in primary
colors like a box of crayons
spilling across grey pavement.
My red-clad girl is ahead of me
in a voting line at a spring
primary on a sunny day.
I wave to her.
She waves in return.
Her first college roommate
a couple of steps ahead
in line waves too
and I guess incorrectly
they are here together.
I wait to talk
to them after voting
but they slip away.
I see my daughter alone
as I'm leaving, collapsed
near a chain-link fence,
her red jacket stark against
dirty broken pavement.
I brake, double park,
run to her side, shake her,
call her name, but she
does not wake. I call 911,
wait with her, hold her,
impatient for help.
St. Elizabeth ER docs
clad in blue scrubs
ask if she takes drugs.

I don't know but
believe she does not,
look in her bag for insulin,
hand it over to them,
explain her other ailments.
Praying she revives
soon, I call our loved ones
to get here fast. Primal fear
for her wakes me in a cold sweat.

It's Not the End

Warm winter days
invite spring dreams

Sticky cinnamon rolls
are best when warm -
sip hot coffee or tea,
wash sugar away

Chewing fingernails
is a sign of distress -
see a counselor,
unburden your mind

Think out-of-the-box,
smile often -
every soul deserves
a happy ending

If you aren't happy,
it's not the end

ADDITIONAL PRAISE FOR *THE LAST YELLOW ROSE*

Juxtaposing memories both light and dark of her family over four generations, Lin Brummels' collection, *The Last Yellow Rose*, offers a sense of the haunting uncertainties in both our genetic makeup and our familial relationships. The dichotomies that arise in the poet's family relationships early on, and the uncertainties that arise with her daughter's ongoing health concerns following a diagnosis of PKU, serve to remind us that we too are products of such uncertain connections.

In these poems, as in life, we are inevitably left with important unanswered questions. The poet reflects on one such question in "Closed Barn Doors," where her mother "told stories about times Harley / took her and her sisters / to the barn to discipline them. / Pressed for details, she always / answered, 'Daddy just tickled us girls.'" Like the poet, the reader is left to wonder about the effect of an episode obviously striking enough to resurface in her mother's stories. And the uncertainty rendered here serves to haunt every reference to her mother in later poems.

As they relate the poet's sense of her family's progression from the years before and during the Great Depression to the present day, these poems view the complex and uncertain relationships that evolve among family members, and they urge us to consider how such relationships, along with our genetics, are something we each carry with us into the future.

   ଔ Neil Harrison, author of for *The Love of God*,2023, *Where the Waters Take You*, 2019 Nebraska Book Honor Poetry Award

Lin Brummels' poems seat me in a sunroom, soft afternoon rays landing on thriving greenery, one a deep pink Christmas cactus in full summer bloom. A sewing machine sits in the corner with red fabric hanging from its needle, like a tongue. The smell of wild yellow roses wafts through the west-facing screens. We sit at a heavy wood table, polished smooth from generational wear of family meals, and over a cup of hot coffee and a plate of warm shortbread cookies, she feeds me deep-set stories of family, as if harvesting damning secrets "with gaps/that must be filled with love." With a sharp inward view of her outlook, Lin's collection feeds and comforts the reader with such intimacy, you will feel that "This is my story too."

ଓ   Bonnie Johnson-Bartee, author of *Cord Blood*, 2023 Nebraska Book Honor Poetry Award

In this exquisite new collection, Lin Brummels invites us to explore the themes of a life on the land and of family—the deep history of love and hurt, stories of "mothering daughters" and "daughtering" mothers. There are stories of hard work and hard luck, but also of the solace of the plains and its beauty. Poignant, bittersweet, sometimes wry, there is wisdom in these pages. This poet tells it like it is, life like the last yellow rose, sweet but with the inevitable barb.

ଓ   Lucy Adkins, author of *A Crazy Little Thing*, 2023 Nebraska Book Award for Poetry

www.ingramcontent.com/pod-product-compliance
Lightning Source LLC
Chambersburg PA
CBHW020210090426
42734CB00008B/1006